Amazon Indian Designs
from Brazilian and Guianan Wood Carvings

Amazon Indian Designs
from Brazilian and Guianan Wood Carvings

HJALMAR STOLPE

DOVER PUBLICATIONS, INC., NEW YORK

Published in Canada by General Publishing Company, Ltd.,
30 Lesmill Road, Don Mills, Toronto, Ontario.
Published in the United Kingdom by Constable and Company,
Ltd., 10 Orange Street, London WC 2.

*Amazon Indian Designs from Brazilian and Guianan Wood
Carvings,* first published by Dover Publications, Inc., in 1974, is
an original selection of designs from the pictorial volume, titled
South America. Atlas, which accompanied the work *Collected
Essays in Ornamental Art by Hjalmar Stolpe* [no publisher, city
or date; printed in 1927 by the Aftonbladets Tryckeri in Stock-
holm; for further bibliographical details, see Publisher's Note].
The selection and layout of the present edition are by Theodore
Menten.

DOVER *Pictorial Archive* SERIES

International Standard Book Number: 0-486-23040-6
Library of Congress Catalog Card Number: 93-92501

Manufactured in the United States of America
Dover Publications, Inc.
180 Varick Street
New York, N.Y. 10014

PUBLISHER'S NOTE

The designs in this book are from rare and exceptionally fine carved wooden objects made by indigenous tribes of Brazil and the Guianas in the nineteenth century, and now dispersed among nearly thirty ethnographic collections in nine European countries. Almost all the objects are war clubs, but there are also a few other items: canes for beating time at dances, rubbing boards for making snuff, flutes and rattles. The designs include human and animal figures and abstract motifs.

The illustrations are reproduced from the pictorial volume, titled *South America. Atlas,* which accompanied the essay "Studies in American Ornamentation. A Contribution to the Biology of Ornament," contained in the volume *Collected Essays in Ornamental Art by Hjalmar Stolpe,* printed in Stockholm in 1927. Stolpe (1841–1905), Director of the Ethnographic Department of the National Museum of Natural History in Stockholm, had originally published that essay in Stockholm in 1896 as "Studier i Amerikansk Ornamentik. Ett Bidrag till Ornamentens Biologi."

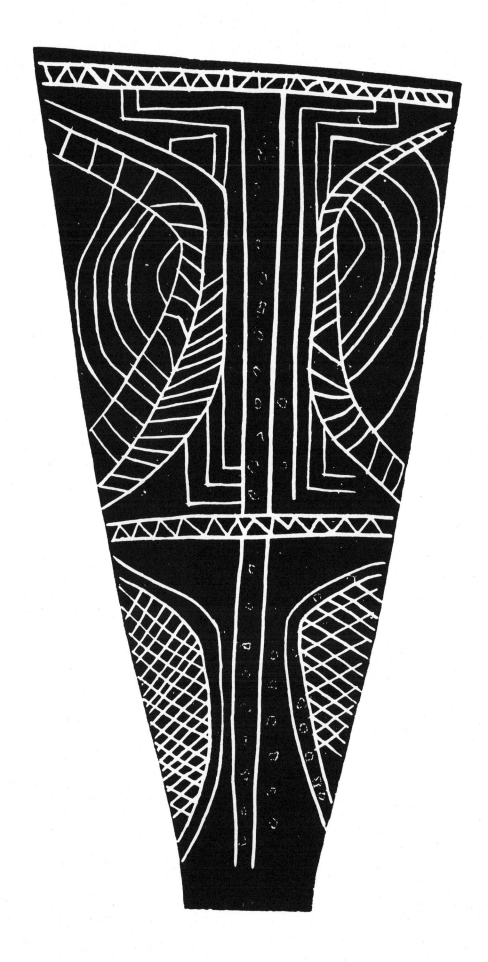

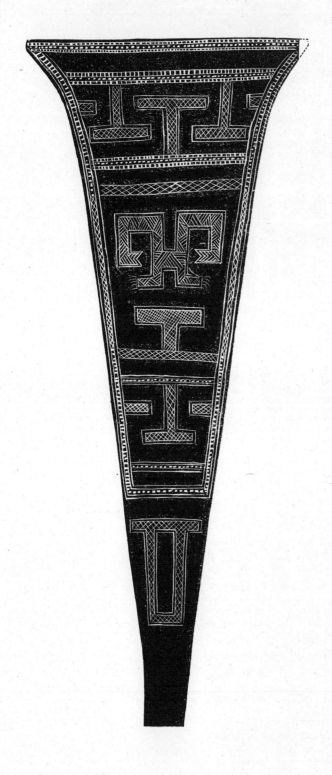

3

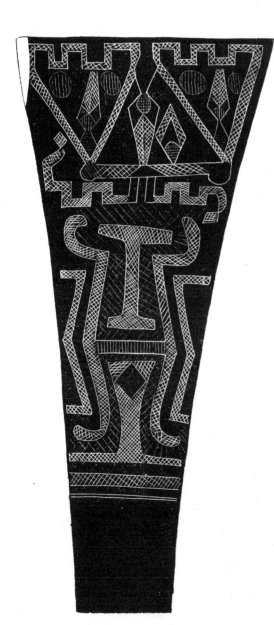

7

8

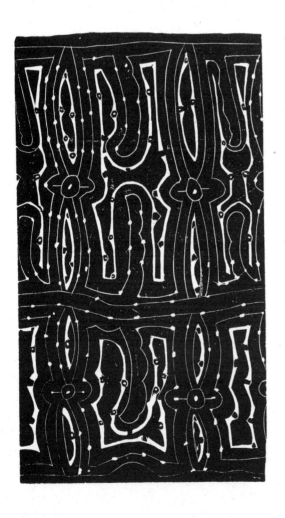

9

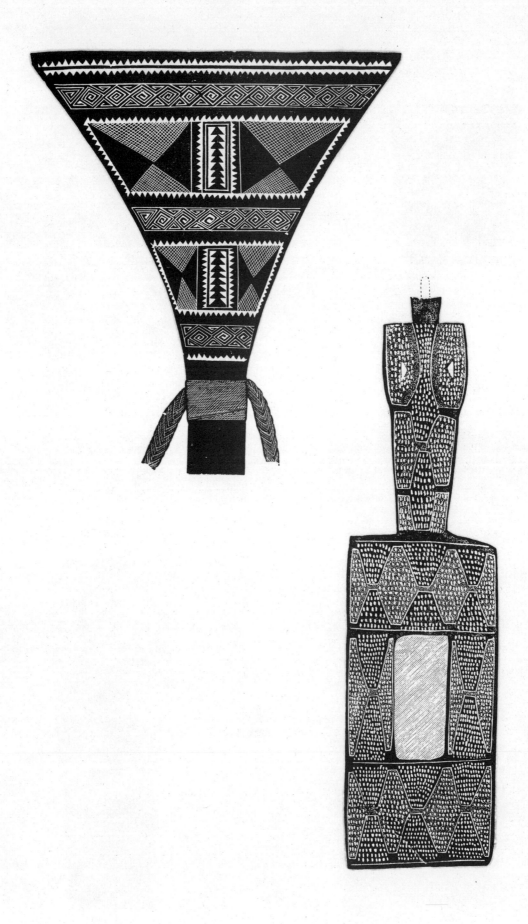

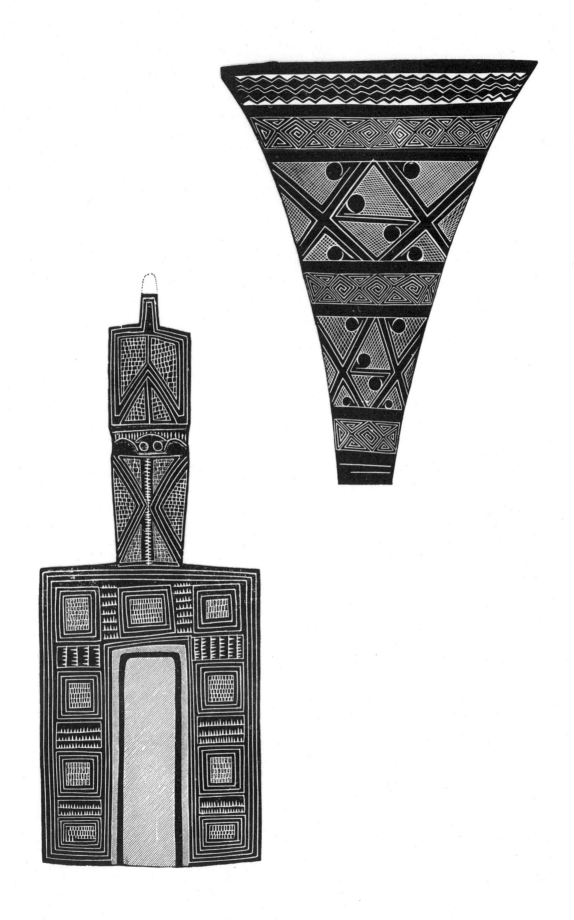

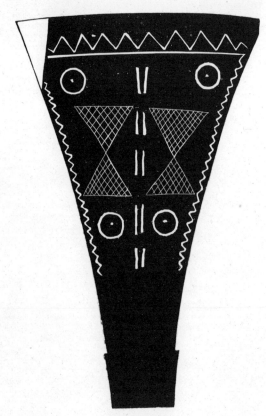

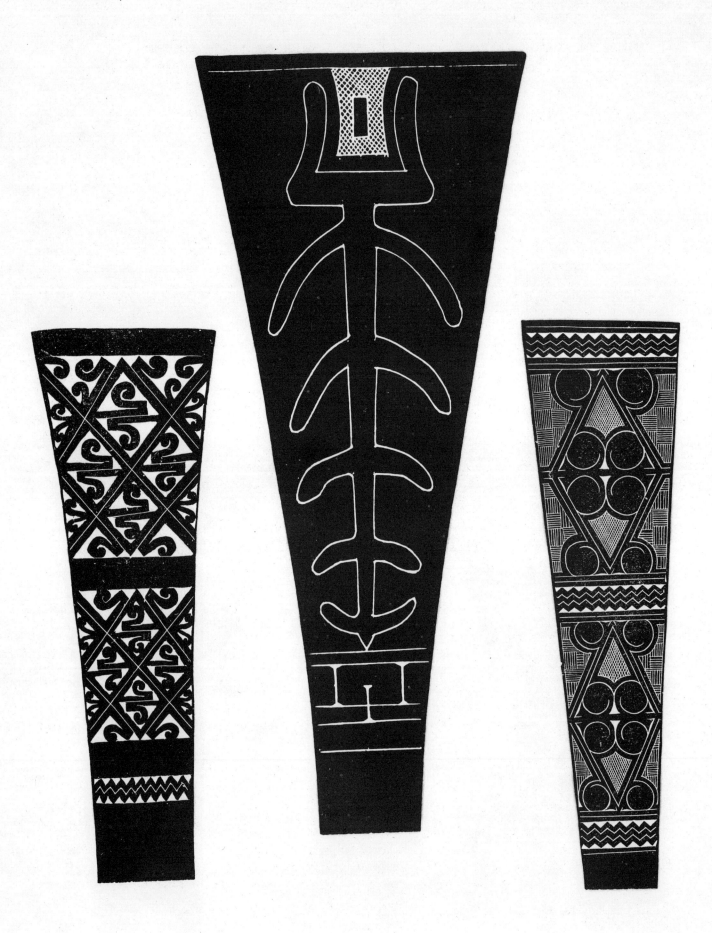

14

17

18

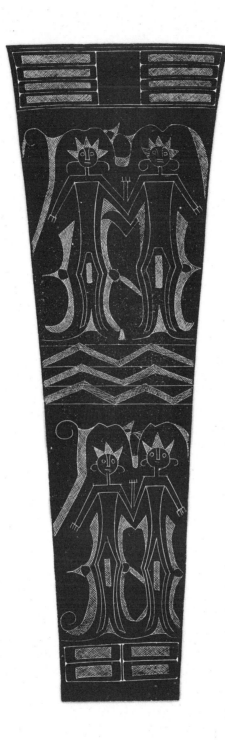

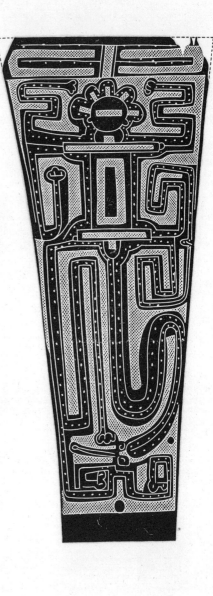

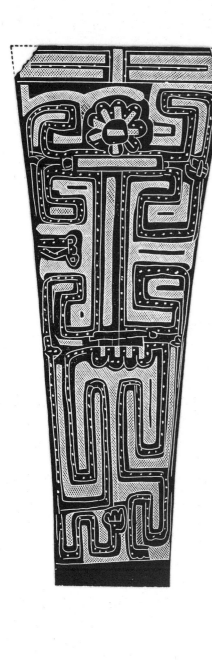

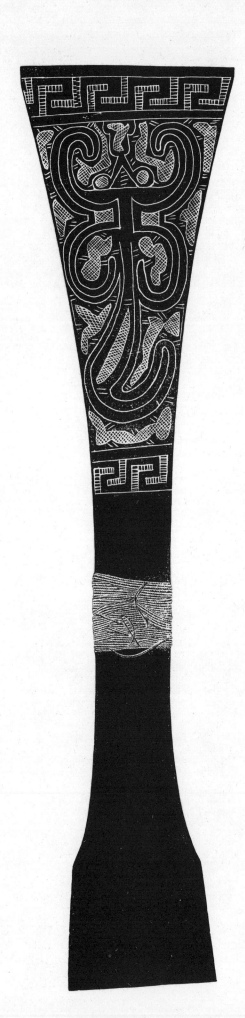

26

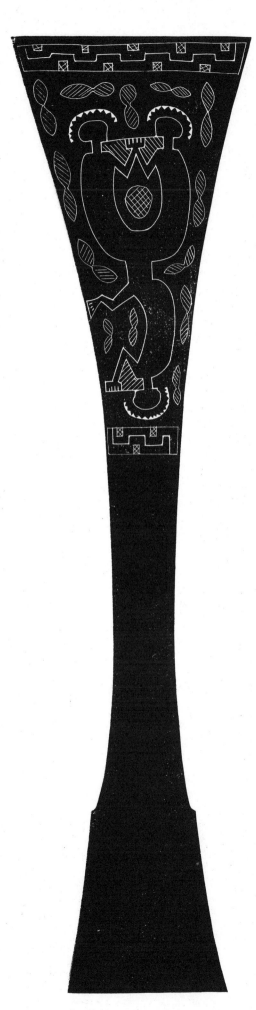

27

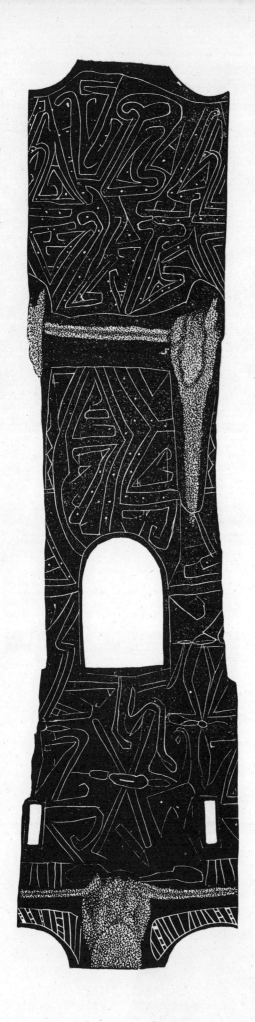

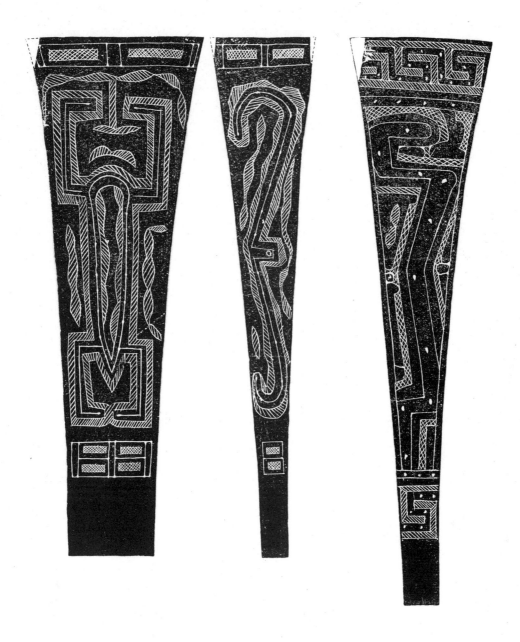

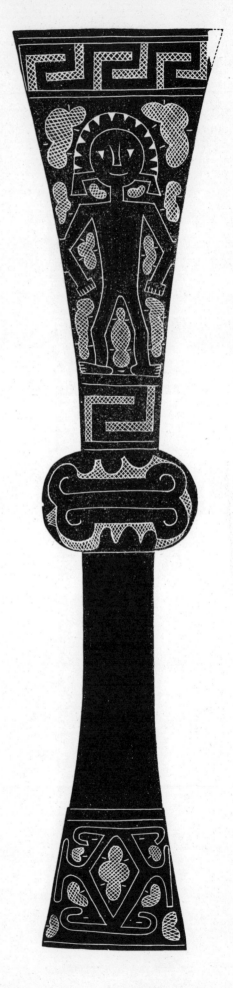

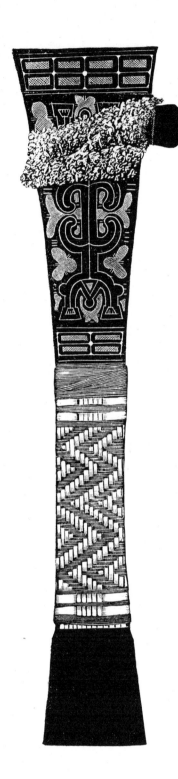

43

44

45

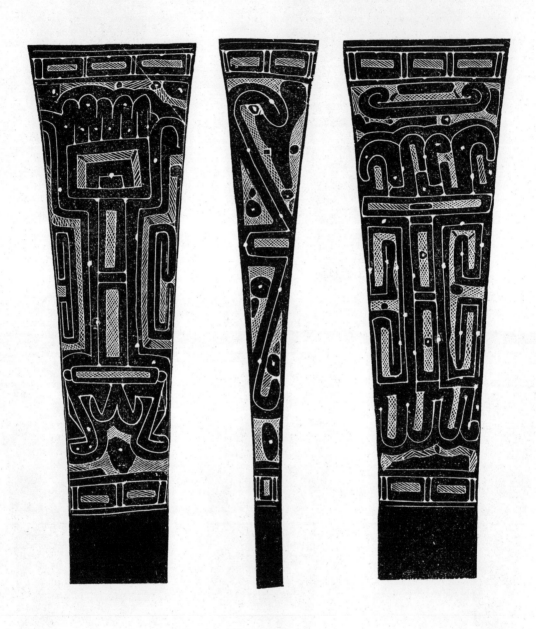

48

52

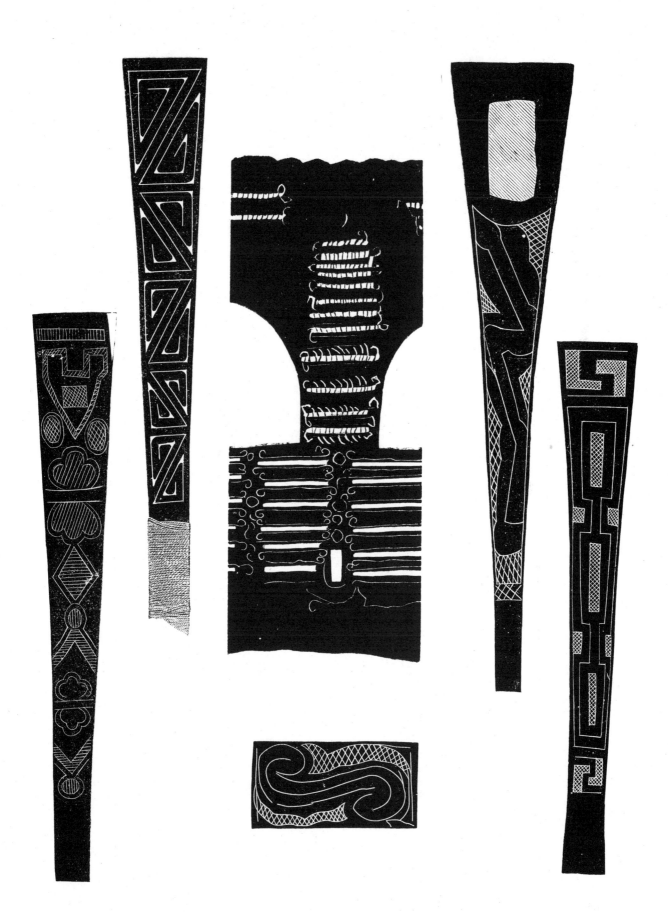

53

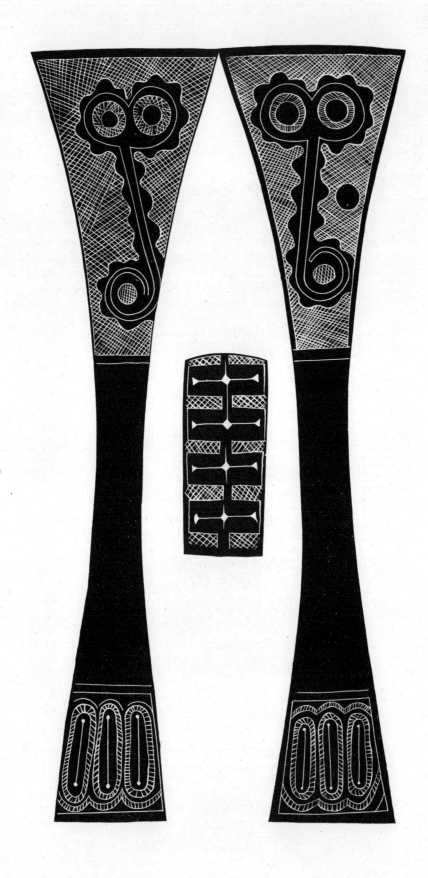